# TRUE
# POWER

CALEB YOUNG

**Effective Use**

**DISCLAIMER:** The material in this book is for informational purposes only. As each individual situation is unique you should use proper discretion in consultation with a health care professional before undertaking the techniques described in this book.

The author and publisher specifically disclaim responsibility for any adverse effects that may result from the use of the information contained in this book.

<u>**Use the brevity of this book to your advantage:**</u> **1) You are only given crucial information; 2) This guide is designed so that you spend less time reading and more time putting what you learn into practice; and 3) It is easy to relocate particularly useful or interesting segments long after you have read them. Be sure to go back and consult the various sections from time to time.**

ISBN: 0987753207
ISBN-13: 9780987753205

Dedicated to my grandfather.

# Contents

*Even if the eyes are afraid, the hands work.*
*– Russian Proverb*

# Chapter I: Introduction

Dear Reader,

I want to begin by congratulating you on taking the important step of obtaining and opening the pages of this guide. Clearly, a part of you is reaching for improvement, motivation and self-management. Not many people take such decisive steps to advance in their own life.

Before we begin, however, you must fully understand that while this guidebook is your companion, it cannot know your goals or the type of person you happen to be. Neither can it respond to your questions – it can only predict them. The real exploration is yours to undergo. As the Chinese proverb so eloquently expresses, "Teachers open the door, but you must enter by yourself."

Within this brief handbook you will find powerful tools and techniques to help you improve your performance in whatever you set out to do.

Whether you have unrealized dreams, debilitating habits, personal problems, or a desire to augment already-existing strengths and success, the information you now hold in your hands can help you rise to entirely new levels of achievement.

For this reason, the book is for *everyone*. While it certainly deals with the notions of success, fulfillment, growth, image and transformation, this guide does not discriminate based on how much or how little you make or who you happen to be in the world. All of us seek happiness and one person aims to accomplish something slightly different than the next. Therefore, based on your goals and effective use of the tool you now hold in your hands, the course of your journey, and your results, will differ from anyone else's.

❧❧

As we move through life, making improvements in quality of life can be difficult, especially with obstacles, inhibitions, setbacks and other forms of resistance that we come across in *every* single thing we set out to accomplish. There are five common outcomes of attempts to make improvements and changes. See if you can relate to any of the following phenomena:

**1. No initiative:** You decide to do something that you know would be good for you but do not follow through. You remain in the planning stage, you spend a lot of time thinking about it, but nothing actually happens, either due to low motivation, low confidence, fear and uncertainty, procrastination, laziness, or poor planning of your daily schedule, leaving you with insufficient drive to tackle the task.

**2. Exhaustion:** You become excited about making a change or pursuing something meaningful to you. Unfortunately, things do not seem to be moving. At best, all your energy is either spent in the first week or two, or something happens that discourages you and sends you plummeting back to a state of exhaustion, frustration and indifference.

**3. Reversion:** This happens quite a lot with people who struggle with poor tendencies: you conquer your bad habit to the point where you think you can handle practicing it again. Due to the slowness and steadiness of the reimplementation of the habit, odds are, you falsely believe that having conquered the habit one time grants you permanent control over it. If you belong in this category, you may also have heard yourself say something like "I can change (or quit) any time I want to."

> **THOUGHT TO RETAIN: Your bad habit is your enemy in war. You cannot call yourself victorious if you conquer the enemy territory only to allow yourself to be overthrown again. When you conquer land, you must also keep it for good. Otherwise you are left with nothing.**

**4. Breaking down:** The starting situation is the same as in the Reversion. The difference is that you plummet to the bottom very quickly from immediate heavy implementation of a bad habit. You slip once, and you go even lower than when you were when you decided to give yourself a chance to change your ways. As well, there is no denial of loss with this one. You know exactly when you fail. You lose all control in a single moment.

**5. True Power:** While the finer details of "success" are defined by you, in this book it means doing your best to have fewer regrets about what could have been, doing so by living more actively and fully: by embarking on a journey in which you challenge yourself and, in meeting those challenges, take calm and decisive action to advance yourself intellectually, culturally, socially and physically. When you become stronger in those ways, you become better, you become a leader, and you become more valued. You will feel an incredible difference and experience the world in a whole new light, not only becoming better equipped to help yourself, but perfectly capable to enrich the lives of those around you.

We all have regrets. We have all said to ourselves at some point in our lives: "I wish I had done things differently" or "I wish I could go back in time and fix everything."

And while learning from the past is important, simply put, regretting the past is impractical. Regret can be an incredibly empowering force, but *only when it is used **in the moment***. These three questions: "What do I want?", "What am I doing?" and "Will what I am doing get me what I want?" can help you project any regret you may have onto the present and assist you not only in mobilizing, but in identifying your current position relative to your goals. The reality is that if you work to minimize your regrets in the present day, you will avoid having regrets of the past. Think about it.

> **THOUGHT TO RETAIN:** The golden rule is that you cannot win unless you play. If you want results, you *have* to put in the work. In times where you are reluctant, you have to *force* or *compel* yourself to work. There is <u>no</u> way around this.

While it is true that you will need to work hard at whatever you set out to accomplish, this guide provides effective ways of going about this. You should be aware that it is possible to *love* meeting challenges and working hard, especially in light of the prospective results. You must also understand that even if by some chance you do not accomplish all that you plan, you may become far more successful from the journey to the goal alone than you will from reaching it. Reflect on this: you <u>will</u> get something exceptionally valuable and unique out of your efforts, even if you do not reach a particular goal. Your True Power will be yours to discover.

❦

**Origins**

I am not the ultimate example of incredible transformation; I have witnessed changes that are far greater than mine and at first I considered sharing them as an alternative to a brief overview of my story, but as the techniques in this guide are a reflection of my life, and to avoid loss of perspective, I realized my side of things cannot be ignored. Still, keep in mind that, in the end, it is all about you.

My story is not uncommon. I was bullied often, from as early as preschool and part way into high school. Not wanting to upset my parents, who dealt with struggles of their own, from the first day my troubles began, I made sure they never saw me saddened or concerned. Unfortunately, shutting out everyone from my problems resulted in anxiety and severe self-esteem issues very early on.

My first acquaintances were kids who chose me for the simple reason that I would do things for them. I listened to them and respected them, even when they disrespected me. I kept my mouth shut about the way I felt in spite of my resentment toward the way I was treated, and I had terrible problems saying no. My self-esteem problems escalated into a strong intolerance to personal criticism as well as an overbearing habit of biting my nails and pulling out my hair. I had suicidal thoughts as early as age 8.

Well into high school, I subconsciously accepted the notion that my problems and faults are a permanent part of my identity. I unintentionally defined myself by my weaknesses; I was the guy who "cannot run that fast", "the guy who is simply not good at math", "the guy who is unattractive", "the guy who is weak", and so on. Yet, surprisingly, the reason things seemed so terrible was still incomprehensible to me. "I am a good person. Why are all these bad things happening to me?"

Even as a senior in high school, I did poorly in my studies and my social life, and I felt like my strength to do anything about my personality and my habits was drained from my body. My grades suffered and morale plummeted. I felt unable to change myself into an organized, punctual and hard-working individual, despite the effort projected by my parents into encouraging and supporting me, and spending what little money they had on tutoring to help my grades and study habits.

I had come to love anything that could help me escape from the reality of failure. I adored the virtual world of computer games primarily because I felt that I could only be successful there, even though such successes were nothing more than an amalgamation of ultimately meaningless accomplishments.

> **THOUGHT TO RETAIN: Luck, success and strength are qualities that gravitate toward positive energy, relentlessness and good role models. When things are dark all around you, do not look around for light when you have the power to become that very light.**

I did not foresee a future. I did not foresee relationships. I did not even want to think about what could happen to me – what awaited me at the bottom of the barrel.

In the back of my mind I knew that, the way things were going, the terrifying prospect of home-lessness was a possibility. After all, my future looked bleak; I had nothing to call a social life; I was extremely weak physically and mentally, had low self-esteem and little self-respect, was sensitive to a crippling fault; had a set of bad habits, compulsions and addictions; and, to top it off, an uncontrollable fear of embarrassment and risk.

❧

It is certainly not a well-kept secret that long-standing bad habits and self-esteem issues acquired from childhood are very difficult to purge. But, as with me, positive change can occur in anyone. So the question is: what happened? What changed?

I remember sitting on the edge of my bed one day and reflecting on my situation, giving myself a much-needed but painful glance at my life.

Following some hours of reflection, I came to the principal realization that my *regret of the past* is unquestionably the most *useless* tool I have in my arsenal of problems. Nevertheless, I could not help but deeply resent the present: the fact that nothing was improving and, most importantly, that I did *nothing* to aid myself.

I recalled the passionate goals for my future that I had as a child: wanting to write, to entertain and to help others; to contribute to those who have become used to living without hope. "What of my goals?" I thought. "I'm not even giving myself a chance! What an awful waste."

The more I thought about those things, the more emotional I became. My mind flew and my heart beat remorselessly. Frustration kicked in and at some point I suddenly felt compelled to do *something*, as if I were pushed into a corner with no option but to fight.

An inexplicable excitement surged within me at the prospect that change was going to occur. I did not know where to aim this excitement and whether or not I would even succeed at whatever I was going to do but, for the first time in my life, I did not care. I did not want to live with my regret anymore. With all my goals and aspirations, with all the sacrifices my parents had made for me, there is *no way* I deserved to live such a sad life. If my life was worth anything, and I knew it had to be, then I better make it count for something.

The question of my physical strength provided me with a starting point. I reasoned that becoming fit physically could be an effective catalyst to improving my confidence and that subsequently tackling the remainder of my problems would become relatively easier.

After months of searching, I hit a part-time job and joined the nearest, least-expensive gym I could find.

I had absolutely no problems working-out regularly. I just got up, did my work-out three times a week, and did so with Calm, Intent and Focus.

The thought of what ran through the minds of other people as they watched me struggle with those 5-pound weights did not stop me from continuing at my own pace because I did not *let* it stop me. Giving into insecurity would only ensure my goals would remain unreached. I sucked it up until I did not care about embarrassment anymore. Neither did I care about the effort needed to bring me to the point of satisfaction, in spite of the fact that

I knew perfectly well that desired results *will* take a long time.

And while the first year did not produce satisfaction, improvement was evident, and so I continued up to this day.

At that time, since I was still experimenting with self-improvement techniques, the majority of the transformation process took *years*. I had slip-ups, I made mistakes – there were periods where I reverted back to the habits – but I learned and developed methods to keep going as I encountered new problems.

I trained myself to accept that I am not the same person anymore, and such thinking seemed to help. I also found that mandatory tasks became easier to handle when I learned to approach them with Calmness, Intent and Focus, just as I had done with going to the gym.

---

**THOUGHT TO RETAIN: Do not be too proud to seek help for yourself, but also be confident in your power to help others.**

---

As time passed, unfavourable habits became manageable, while the most terrible were obliterated to the point of repulsion. My self-esteem and sociability improved to an amazing degree; I became more organized and athletic; I found good friends; and my grades went up dramatically. I certainly worked a lot harder to keep this up, but the undeniable fact is that I *loved* to work hard because I *loved* the opportunities and the refreshing life my busy schedule had awarded me. I loved not having regrets; I loved the prospect of not having them for the rest of my life. If you would have told the "old me" this sort of change was a possibility, I would not have believed you.

Interestingly enough, I did not think of sharing the methods I used to achieve these results until years later.

A friend called me out one evening to the university pub. As the time passed, the manner of our conversation became progressively personal. He revealed frustrations about an array of matters: no girlfriend, poor performance in his team sport, feelings of low-energy and stress, tardiness, tendencies to skip classes, and a dreadful sense of uncertainty in regards to the future.

His concerns had me taken aback. The man was intelligent, attractive, and in incredible shape – not an individual expected to harbour such concerns, no matter how mundane.

I illustrated to him techniques by the virtue of which I dealt with similar problems in the past, and the way in which these methods help me with often

unavoidable personal issues, including relationships, loss of loved ones, and other factors of self-
management. He said he would try the methods
despite my expressed doubt of their effectiveness.
I reasoned that what may have worked for me may
not work for someone else. Nevertheless, I could
tell that he was serious in his intention to change
and I wished him well.

After a surprisingly brief period, he reflected
positive changes and, having confirmed that my
advice had helped, I freed the knowledge to people
close to me. The recipients of this information were
a small group of people of different sexes, ages and
backgrounds.

Naturally, not everyone took my words into
practice, not all needed them, but those who used
the knowledge became noticeably less inhibited by
factors such as low self-esteem, regret and mental
blocks. To them, the process of self-improvement
and exploration became almost like a game, and
failure had only one definition: not playing. It was
as if a new, interesting world unfolded before their
eyes.

The sharing of these powerful methods of self-
transformation brought about a sort of pact, in
which each practitioner of these techniques vowed
not to let unreasonable fears keep them from finding success, living life more fully, and being good

role models for others. The idea of a pact was a very advantageous arrangement because it gave all people involved a sense of belonging, pride, and motivation not to give up. This way, even if we were miles apart, neither one of us would ever be alone. Fundamentally, success is more easily attained when a person has a sense of belonging; progress can be difficult to achieve in a state of solitude.

❦

To this day, we all had hurdles to overcome in our ongoing journeys, and we are always finding new things we want to experience, new challenges we want to undertake, and new things we want to see. We wish each other health and happiness, because what more does one need?

I was speaking to another close friend over the phone one night, and he said to me: "You should bring more people into this." Then he chuckled.

Something clicked.

I was touched by my friends' successes and I sensed in my heart that it should not end with my family and friends. Leaving it there would be just another waste of what my life had produced. Knowing that there *are* people out there with a potential unfulfilled only as a result of behavioural issues such as low self-esteem was enough reason for me to write this guidebook. Such people have the potential to become happier and more successful, no matter their profession, sex, income, age, past history or lifestyle.

In the next two chapters, I will share three techniques with you: Release, Ghost Training, and Power Word. And in the last two chapters, you will find effective ways to keep track of your progress and, ultimately, basic but crucial notes, step-by-step, on proper sleeping and waking.

---

**THOUGHT TO RETAIN: Life is an adventure. Do not be discouraged if you start at the bottom: the harder the journey being conquered, the greater the chance for magnificent change to take place. Use your position to your advantage.**

---

We still have faults (everyone does), we are not 100% "productive" (nobody is), we still make time to relax (have to smell the roses, right?), we still have things we need to improve (opportunities to get even stronger), but we are progressing with Calm, Intent and Focus.

Things may be slow sometimes, they may be fast at other times, but we are *always* on the move. And we love it.

*When the way comes to an end, then change–*
*having changed, you pass through. – I Ching*

# Chapter II: Release

> **THOUGHT TO RETAIN:** Do not give up if things go terribly wrong. Even failure can grant you tremendous power and confidence if you immediately take action to regain composure. No matter what, get up and continue in whatever way you can, using the resources you have at your disposal.

Depending on what you have set out to do, your journey may be more difficult than someone else's, which may raise doubt in regard to the probability of success. Still, the odds are spectacularly in your favour, together with the likelihood that you will surpass your own expectations.

**The Release Technique** is a mental exercise that is intended to increase self-esteem by "releasing" yourself from the parts of your personality that harbour thoughts of negative self-image in order to change poor habits (*non-addiction*, such as tardiness), personality traits that are untrue to your true self, and cripplingly self-deprecating views on your own position in the world.

❦

**Initiating and Understanding the Release**

The first principle is **to acknowledge what you want to improve.** If you are unsure, listen to your intuition. It will tell you what you need to change. Be honest with yourself. Is it related to your career? Health? Relationships? Attitude?

If you have a bad habit that seems relatively mild or "insignificant", do keep it in mind as something to improve. Let me give you an example of why you should do this:

I was a messy person most of my life. I did not mind living in a mess as much as I do now. When my social life improved, I still found myself very reluctant to invite people into my home, and for good reason: it was never prepared for company. It shut out potential friends as well as relationships.

As a result of my disorganized behaviour, I was frequently late for work, I got into trouble, stayed late to make up time and subsequently had no energy to do anything else, let alone watch television when I could not locate the remote. My own home – ideally a place capable of accommodating both relaxation and work – drained my energy and wasted my time. In such a way, an issue that I deemed "insignificant" held me back significantly.

The second principle: **Release yourself using the mindset that does not have the problem you are dealing with. To do this, implement Calmness, Intent and Focus.**

When you feel you are bad at something – for example, from experience or from what someone might have said or implied – you identify with that idea about yourself and it becomes absorbed into your identity, influencing your personality, your health, your energy and your fears. This becomes "the mindset that has the problem" – the very same mental state you are most likely trying to change.

One of the biggest mistakes people make when trying to improve themselves is making their transformation using that very crippling mindset.

When you use that mindset, you are hurting your chances of successful change. In effect, the transformation becomes a struggle because you remain in your old self while trying to remove your old self.

This approach causes failure every single time. Think about it: if you continue to identify yourself with an idea that you are bad at something, how can you expect to improve your performance? You end up burning out, losing motivation and going nowhere.

Do not enter into a struggle with yourself in which you desperately try to control the thoughts of negative self-image. Instead, change your entire being, your essence, into someone with a positive self-image. Let go.

---

**A great approach to anything related to self-management or tasks which may be difficult, including changing your mindset, is exercising the combination of Calmness, Intent and Focus:**

1. **Calmness: A state free of panic, worry and self-doubt achieved by meditation, controlled breathing, or controlled venting of worrisome emotion. Calmness preserves your energy for Intent and Focus.**
2. **Intent: 100% intention to win and, conversely, absolutely no intention to lose.**
3. **Focus: *Identifying your identity with the Intent, <u>and</u> acting upon your Intent with Calmness.***

---

As an example, the sudden change in the effort that I made to become a better student, all those years ago, was a very calm and intentional choice. While the road was not easy, the pursuit for that high GPA was very decisive. I had a strong intention to win, and I was calm partly due to the fact that I stopped myself from sitting there thinking about winning (as if I had already succeeded without lifting a finger) and riling myself up, because that would be wasting energy. Instead I used that energy to *act* to satisfy my Intent. I worked very hard – an unavoidable part of guaranteed success – *but,* working that hard had never been so easy to implement. My poor study habits did not matter anymore; it felt great to bring out that true side of me. It is a wonderful feeling advancing to a new level.

A similar release materialized with an acquaintance. In three years after graduating from college, he secured only two part-time minimum wage jobs, at which he worked no more than four months before quitting each one. What is worse, in that three-year period, less than a day was spent on job-hunting! At some point, he simply became fed up with the concept of losing and went out, tackled the job hunt, survived rejections, kept moving forward, and after a few months nailed a full-time job. He was calm, focused and committed to victory.

☯

## The Release in Detail

> **THOUGHT TO RETAIN: You will notice that
> in the tobacco-addiction story in the following
> section, my grandfather uses the Power Word
> in *combination* with the Release Technique.
> When dealing with overcoming any sort of ad-
> diction, do <u>NOT</u> practice this particular tech-
> nique without also using *Power Word* or *Ghost
> Training*, featured in the following chapter.**

Absorbed in my own problems, I did not realize
the value of having witnessed the Release in action
until I inadvertently implemented it in my own
transformation later in life. I first noticed the Release Technique in action on my grandfather nearly
twenty years ago:

I remember him standing on the veranda and
my mother urging: "Dad, stop smoking! You have
to quit!" I was right there in the yard, observing
him puffing on his cigarette. I could tell he was
struggling – the resistance was written on his face.
The pressure annoyed him, but it was obvious that
he loathed the habit.

He stood staring into nowhere, inhaled the
smoke once more, took a deep breath, clenched
his teeth, and put out the cigarette in the ashtray.

That was the last time he touched a cigarette. And this was a sixty-three year old man who smoked from his early teens.

When I thought about it later, in my own journey, how someone like my grandfather could quit and never smoke again, I recalled some notable details: whenever his buddies would offer him a cigarette, he would refuse and say: "Sorry, I don't smoke."

They would tease: "Oh come on. Are you trying to quit?"

And he would reply: "I'm not trying to do anything. I'm simply not a smoker. It does not interest me."

Those details are important. He did not say "I'm trying to quit"; he did not even talk about "quitting". He straightforwardly uttered "I'm not a smoker" and implied that cigarettes repulse him. It all looked so easy from the side.

A year ago, I spoke with him about this experience. He confessed the obvious. Stopping smoking was not easy. He had occasional withdrawal-symptoms; headaches, irritation, restlessness. He sought medical help when he felt it was necessary and did exercises to keep *calm*, but he got through it. He made it a point to remind himself that he is not a smoker; he uttered the words **"I will not be defeated"** (reflection of his *Intent*, and his "Power

Word") whenever he felt he was slipping; and he made a conscious choice to *never* smoke casually. The habit was utterly obliterated from his identity – and today he wears this story as a badge of victory. Considering he did not have the self-management tools we have today, his is an incredible accomplishment.

☯

## Recognizing Success of Release

One concern someone expressed to me about this technique: *"Do you honestly expect me to become a different person altogether? You seem to be implying that I force myself to forget my past. It does not seem natural or realistic."*

If you are to take anything away from this guide, it should be the realization that you are changing *all the time.* Every event, every new experience, transforms you. This is true even as you are reading these words. And over the course of your life, you may become an entirely different person. And if you are improving through the changes, your transformation ought to be embraced, not avoided.

Even if you become different, by no means does this imply forgetting your past, your history and your journey through life; letting go of your past and forgetting your past are *not* one and the same. Think about it this way:

Have you had a situation that you recall used to hurt you emotionally but hurts no longer? Why does it not bother you anymore?

The answer is simple: you are not the same person; it was an old self that had the problem.

Upon deeper reflection you will realize that you are a different person not from having had the issue, but from the fact that you are no longer affected by it in the same way as when you *identified yourself with it*. In slang terms, you are "over it". You have not forgotten the past, but you feel as if the issue has separated from you. The Release aims to emulate the *exact* same feeling of being "over" your issue. And, we all agree, there is nothing unnatural about this feeling, even when you take charge of your transformation to attain it.

If at any point in using the Release you still do not feel like you are successfully "getting over" something, test yourself: when you are using this technique, is it easier to mobilize? To get things done? If so, then you are doing just fine. Otherwise, just keep practicing. Ultimately, embrace and enjoy the power this technique brings out from within you. Feel good to be different. Embrace change.

**THOUGHT TO RETAIN:** Take the opportunity to empower your new self. If your old self could not handle certain issues or problems, your new self can do so with extreme ease. Use this mindset to your advantage.

*I am a writer who came from a sheltered life. A sheltered life can be a daring life as well. For all serious daring starts from within. – Eudora Welty*

# Chapter III: Ghost Training and the Power Word

Hopefully you have been able to grasp the premise of the Release. Otherwise, not to worry, you can always come back to that section again.

It is important to understand the roles of the different techniques so you have a clear goal in mind in regards to why you are using the technique and what you wish to achieve as part of your *Intent*. While the Release alters your state of mind, it may or may not be enough to give you the courage and motivation to act *in the moment*.

One of the most expressed desires of people with addictions, bad habits or fear is a mentor or coach to be next to them at all times to control them. It would be wonderful to have someone with you to slap the cigarette out of your hand each time you try to light up or to have someone encourage you to work when you are feeling hopeless or push you to take that risk you know would be good for you when you are afraid. Most of the time, we do not have anyone standing next to us to keep us in check. We are left with our self-doubt, our struggles and our fears. The fact is, if someone knocked that cigarette out of your hand each and every time you tried to smoke, you *would* quit. If someone pushed you hard enough to go out of your comfort zone, you *would* do it.

**Ghost Training** and the **Power Word:** two incredibly powerful tools that will help you get that treatment. These techniques help you do things *you know you should* but cannot do as a result of fear, habit, uncertainty, indifference or poor self-esteem and, conversely, control things *you know you should not do* but do anyway for the same reasons.

☙❧

**Ghost Training**

Ghost Training serves two purposes. First, it demonstrates the extent to which your own mind and negative thinking gets in the way of accomplishment and decisive action. Second, it increases confidence and daring.

The best way to learn is to practice, so we will get right into the training.

First thing you should do is think of a fairly simple physical motion or feat. You can select something along the lines of drawing an image or juggling tennis balls. Do not choose something potentially dangerous or strenuous. This is a mental exercise, not a physical one. It is important, however, that the nature of the activity should allow for progress to be seen, felt or measured.

The physical motion I use for when I practice Ghost Training is touching my toes. So, for the sake of example, let us assume that very exercise.

You can go ahead and stand up now. Reach toward your toes. Get a feel of how far down you can go comfortably. If you cannot touch your toes, do not worry.

Now, imagine for a moment that there is a ghost inside of you: your spirit, your inner self. Visualize that this ghost is a lot more powerful than you are and can do a lot that you cannot do physically. In this case, you are going to train your ghost to touch his or her toes:

You can do this with eyes open or closed. Keep your mind calm and relax your face. As you stand, feel your ghost slowly stepping forward out from where your body is standing, and then feel and visualize the ghost bending over and touching its toes. Make sure you visualize this sequence in the exact manner that you would want to touch your toes. Meaning, do *not* picture *only* the end result. Picture the *entire process*: the bending down and the touching of the toes. Visualize this once or twice. As soon as you are done the visualization, reach for your toes as before.

You may still be unable to touch your toes but you should be able to see, feel or measure a noticeable improvement in performance, even if slight. It is incredible what you can do when you put your mind to it.

You must understand that your overall barrier consists of *mental* barriers too, not just the physical. When you remove some of the mental barriers, you can see how much they keep you from performing better at whatever you set out to accomplish. With the Ghost Training, you are able to deal with and decrease your physical barriers and have reasonable confidence to tackle interviews, speaking to people, writing exams; intimacy; performance in sports; performance in the arts; and anything positive that will steer to improvement. The possibilities are endless.

Visualize your ghost's success, and then do it yourself! Just like follow-the-leader.

> **THOUGHT TO RETAIN:** The best way to grow can be as simple as embracing situations that put you out of your comfort zone, in spite of your insecurities and fears.

✎

## Developing Your Power Word

The Power Word is meant to compel you. It is another wonderful technique that serves as an alternative to Ghost Training. While some claim that Ghost Training is superior, you should do what you find works best for what you wish to accomplish. We are all different and therefore one technique may suit you better than another. With time, you may even find yourself modifying the methods to suit your style. It is all about preference. While the Power Word takes more time to develop and become accustomed to, for me it served as the *most* influential self-empowerment technique in my arsenal. I used it *a lot.*

To begin, please give yourself a comfortable amount of time to marinate on the following:

Try to remember what it feels like to be confident, strong, able – or, better yet, bring up the emotion at the moment when you felt most strong, most motivated, and most confident. If you cannot think of a time, shut your eyes and imagine an event that would make you feel most strong, able and confident.

If you still cannot make such a recollection, do not despair. Try a light exercise or do any physical activity that would help your cardiovascular system and release endorphins: jogging, walking, boxing/shadow boxing, or hitting the gym.

At the emotional peak of either the memory or your chosen activity, when you feel most happy and satisfied, select a word or a short phrase to associate to the positive emotion being felt. Decide on something uplifting and unforgettable that will resonate with you.

Do not spend too much time picking out a word. You can even select the first word, phrase or sound that comes to mind. A young woman I know picked the name of her cat as her Power Word and she has done very well with it. Someone else picked his spirit animal. And I am sure somebody out there chose the name of their mother, child or someone they love, because that name, when said aloud, serves as a powerful reminder to that person *not to light that cigarette*, for example.

The greater the connection of the word or phrase to the positive emotion, the more powerful the effects of the technique. **This word or phrase becomes your Power Word.**

❧

Though I only recognized it as a universal technique after hearing the full extent of my grandfather's cigarette story, I had already used the Power Word for some time prior to that.

My Word first came to me when a friend dragged me to a boxing class. As I hit the focus mitts, my training partner cried "straight" … "straight"… "cross"… and I started saying "go", "go", "go" for him to continue stepping back as I rolled with the punches. This was the peak of my feeling the most strong and able and the word "go", associated with these wonderful feelings, became my Power Word. Since then, I have used it hundreds of times and it never failed to compel me to the right action.

It had done wonders for me in school, for example. In university, whenever I felt too lazy to study, I would say my Power Word aloud. As if a switch had been flicked inside of me, I would turn off the television and without *any* hesitation walk over to my desk and start studying. No questions, no complaints, only action.

❧

The technique has four operational requirements for it to work, in proper order of usage:

1) You must have understood and practiced Ghost Training
2) You must want to improve, enhance performance, develop good habits or drop bad ones, and/or overcome fear.
3) The Power Word must be said out loud when you feel you need help (for example, when you are just about to light up a cigarette); and
4) You have to submit to the Power Word (as a continuation of the example in step 3, *immediately* after you say it, you have to stop the process of lighting up **no matter what**, **even if you do not like it, even if you feel you are about to cry. Just stop what you are doing the moment you say it**).

Like Ghost Training, it also works in compelling yourself to attend that dance class, deal with your dental appointment, get something off your chest, exercise, go out and meet new people and so on. **Say** your power word, **listen** to it, and **submit** to it: just go and do it *immediately*. Does not matter if you like it or not because you will love it when you realize the mind-blowing levels of power this technique can grant you, when you let it.

*It is good to have an end to journey toward; but it is the journey that matters in the end. – Ursula K. Le Guin*

# Chapter IV:
# Documenting Your Journey

For millennia, people have been recording their stories and accomplishments. Among such people were great thinkers, explorers and other important figures. Upon close review, you will find that numerous of these accounts are, in their own right, journals of day by day progress, observation and thought.

Moreover, such recordkeeping was not done exclusively for posterity. Journals served as powerful motivating tools, making even the most frightening journeys bearable, by allowing the writer to break down the course of the voyage into smaller manageable steps, one day at a time. It is no wonder many distinguished people use online journals or blogs to keep track of their progress. Doing so makes their busy and stressful lifestyles a *lot* easier on the morale.

It is to your advantage to document your journey as well. The level of detail, of course, is left up to you.

You can purchase a journal or logbook from your local stationary store or make an online journal of your progress.

If you do not already own a calendar, you may want to obtain one and hang it in an easily-accessible space. Make sure the calendar features images that inspire and motivate you.

---

**THOUGHT TO RETAIN: Uncertainty and fear are common feelings that many people experience when making changes to their careers and in learning new skills, especially if the changes place them out of their comfort zone. Minimize your risk however you can, but do not give up on your potential. Start working toward your goals *right away*, even if you start small and progress slowly. You will feel good when you start.**

---

**The War Game: Calendar**

The following is a challenging game involving your calendar and it delivers excellent additional aid to those who feel that it would be easier to achieve their goals on stricter terms. This game is an aggressive and powerful tool that works to ensure that you conduct an activity or duty regularly and according to plan.

Conversely, it works very well for those who wish to pursue a tracking method of purging bad habits (ones driven by addiction especially) from their system.

Before you begin, however, please remember to use the tools in this guide. Give yourself encouragement. Tell yourself "I can do it", "This is easy", and "I won't be defeated." Make sure also to **stay away** from anything sad or depressing. If you do all that, the intensity of this game will be a million times easier to handle.

Begin when ready.

As soon as you start, consider yourself at war with your arch-enemy: your bad habit, for example. So if you were a smoker, from now on you no longer practice smoking, _ever_.

At the beginning, the calendar should be empty of any markings. This means you have not conquered any of your enemy's territory. Naturally, your job is to conquer as much of it as possible. It works like this:

Whatever bad habit or addiction you have chosen to eliminate, draw a big "W" (for "Win") on every day of the calendar that you do not practice the bad habit. As the calendar is filled up with W's, you conquer the territory of your enemy.

In addition to conquering territory, you have regular objectives to accomplish. On every date of the calendar that has the number 9, treat yourself to something different and tasty (use your best judgment if you are using this method to avoid certain foods). On every date that has the number 1, try a new activity. And on every date that has a 6, get together with a friend.

Those are just examples, so the way you choose to reward yourself is up to you, as long as it does not interfere with that which you have been working to avoid.

---

**Take it one day at a time. Remember this for each day you play War: all you have to do is to win today. If you can do this, then you can win tomorrow. Play with Calmness, Focus and Intent.**

---

When you play this game, your journal can also serve as your War Journal: make a record of how *each day* goes for you. This is especially important in the first two or three weeks, when change is most difficult to achieve.

Once the month is full of W's, write an extra entry in your War Journal about what you have accomplished and your goals for next month.

The game ends when you no longer want to practice the bad habit you fought to eliminate, or when you have succeeded in practicing the good habit you have fought to adapt into your schedule.

**Please be aware that once you leave this bad habit and defeat it, you are not to give up your territory to the habit again.**

☺☺

## Accomplishing an Incredible Lot: Schedule

It is said that if you want something done fast and done well, give the task to the busiest individual you can find. Why? The busiest person is the only one who has practiced the art of prioritization. Such a person accomplishes more in the day.

If you hand over the assignment to somebody with loads of free time, expect things to be put off.

Before going to bed, write an agenda for the following day. As an example, you may include:

1) Try fencing class,
2) Look for work and apply for at least fifteen positions,
3) Call insurance company,
4) Book dentist appointment,
5) Go to the gym,
6) Sign up for a workshop.

You get the idea.

When you get up, after breakfast, consult your agenda *immediately* and start working on it with Calmness, Intent and Focus. Get the most time-consuming tasks done first. *There is a strong possibility that you will end up with more time than you expected considering how much you will accomplish.* You will feel incredible.

*Look, children,*
*Hail-stones!*
*Let us rush out!*
*-Basho*

# Chapter V: The Phase of Rest

It is no secret that in dealing with emotional tribulation, poor management of your rest has the potential to *destroy your day*, increasing depression, lowering positive and healthy self-image and decreasing chances of success.

For people under stress or depression, there is a tendency to sleep in. The permeating feeling is the desire to remain under the covers, and for some this emotion comes in the form of not wanting to be awake at all. It is not uncommon for some people to be having their first meal of the day by the time someone else would have finished their second or third. When wakefulness finally comes, the individual feels the burden of fatigue and frustration in spite of the fact they spent so many hours in bed.

In any case, prospects of a productive day are either nonchalantly put off or discarded completely, and the entire day becomes broken. Chances are, in such cases, duties such as your job might quite literally constitute an entire day. As a result, it is no surprise that the day brings neither enjoyment nor productivity. If there is no happiness, restfulness, or a sense of pride about your day, or if you feel sluggish and low-energy, see a health professional. It might simply be a question of modifying your diet or exercise regimen. Your well-being is priority.

⊙⊙

**Night Regeneration**

**Part 1:** Make sure that your sleeping schedule follows a steady pattern. If possible, sleep no later than 11:30pm.

At around midnight, your body begins a process of regeneration and cleansing but you need to be asleep for this process to have the best effect. This is the time when a lot of the toxins are removed from your body, a process which can improve your appearance and overall health for the next day. People who stay up late all the time often have worse skin (in cases where the condition is caused by toxins) than those who allow their body to rest during this crucial period of strengthening and regeneration. People who get proper sleep tend to look more refreshed, younger, stronger, and more attractive than had they slept past midnight.

Make sure to get an appropriate amount of sleep for your age. Not too much, not too little.

**Part 2:** Going to sleep.

a) Change into comfortable sleeping clothes. Prepare your bed for sleep. Some people prefer to lift the cover to make the bed more inviting.

b) Set your alarm for a reasonable time; make sure to get an alarm the ring of which is an enjoyable sound to you! Do not get a clock that is so annoying it ticks you right off every morning. Use a sound that will help motivate you, wake you, and make you smile. If you feel like you can start sleeping at this point, get right into bed. If not, move on to step c.

c) Set the kettle and make yourself a honey-lemon tea or something hot and soothing.

Add real honey. Avoid coffee, green tea, black tea or any beverage that contains high amounts of caffeine or excess amounts of sugar.

d) Set the temperature in the room to a comfortable one (if applicable) and dim the lights if you can. If possible, make sure there is enough fresh air coming in from the outside that will be enough not to disturb your comfort too greatly. Your body will benefit from the fresh air as it regenerates and renews itself when you sleep.

e) If you still feel restless, do some light yoga exercises. Stretch your limbs and your back. Do it slowly and focus on your breathing. Meditate. Listen to meditative and calm music. Do this until your mind is quiet.

f) Go into bed and close your eyes. Trust your body to take care of falling asleep. Do not concern yourself with whether you will fall asleep or not. Take whatever sleep your body gives you. Relax and give it total trust.

## Awakening the Mind

When it is time for you to get up, open your eyes. *Do not* continue sleeping for 15 minutes, 30 minutes or an hour extra, even if you have spare time.

> **THOUGHT TO RETAIN: A consistent sleeping schedule will have a good effect on sleeping as well as waking, which positively influences your sense of well-being the following day. If your sleep is broken or you feel that you need to rest sometime during the day, take a nap. Avoid sleeping-in.**

## Awakening the Spirit

You may be able to use the Ghost technique or the Power Word to compel yourself to get out of bed, but in a sleepy state this simply may not occur to you.

Think about this for a moment: When you wake up, what do you see? Do you see a white wall? Do you see an alarm clock? Do you see a project you need to complete? Do you see a debilitating day ahead of you? The solution is visual material.

Put up a poster, symbol or wall scroll on your wall or wherever it will be visible from your bed, so that when you wake up it will be one of the first things you see when you open your eyes in the morning. Use a meaningful picture of something to which you have a personal connection that you know will contribute to your mentorship:

1) The image can be your Power Word, or something associated with it.
2) It can be your personal hero or someone you admire, even if he or she is fictional.

You may not be able to decide on the visual material right away, but keep looking for that which works for you. All the more so, you can redecorate your room to create an atmosphere that will help you start the day feeling good. Treat it as a quest of self-discovery.

☙❧

**Awakening the Body**

> **THOUGHT TO RETAIN: You can get up and start your day before being fully awake. Being sleepy in the morning does not necessarily mean that you require more sleep.**

Once you see your motivational material, to prepare you, all you need to do is fulfill the following two steps to get out of bed in the best manner:

**Step 1:** Stretch in bed. Do not jump out of bed. Remember that your muscles shut down in your sleep. Your heart is still rested. Keep your eyes *open* while you do this.

Wiggle your toes, flex your calves, wiggle your knees, flex your thighs, flex your stomach, slowly roll your shoulders, and gently elongate your back. Take a minute or two to do the whole stretching process. Roll onto the side from which you will be getting out of bed, get your feet out from under the covers and onto the floor, then gently sit up on your bed and slowly stand up.

Once at this stage, do *not* go back into bed. If you are cold, put on something warm.

**Step 2:** Wash up (use cool, but not cold, water on the face), make breakfast, do what you have planned. If you have to leave for work, account for the time you need to get ready for the commute. If you are unemployed and are looking for work, here is your chance to start bright and early. Remember your inspiration and go for it. If you chose a hero for your poster, *become* the productive and heroic person you admire. Be ready to do great things and inspire others to do the same.

Here you are, at the beginning of a great journey to seek your True Power. From the beginning, you had your goals, your wits, and a lot of potential. Now, you carry newfound knowledge to aid you:

The Release, to move past your insecurities. Ghost Training and Power Word, to compel yourself to act in the moment. The Journal, War Game, and Schedule, to document and keep track of your progress.

Proper sleep and waking, to maintain your energy.

# Chapter VI: For Special Consideration

Whenever you are able, it is great to approach
any kind of difficulty with Calmness and Focus;
Calmness to contain your energy and Focus to aim
the energy to complete the task at hand.

❦

A relatively well-known technique that people have
talked about for years: pretend a television screen
is hovering over your head. This screen showcases
your fears, poor self-esteem, and whatever you
think about yourself to everyone around you. Try to
change what is on that screen.

❦

Keep little notes and reminders of your goals. If you want to remind yourself to floss, for example, put a note in the bathroom. It is that simple.

❧

You may not know the future, but there is no harm in trying to make it better. What will you lose by trying when you can spend so much time regretting not trying at all? You have something good to contribute. Don't know what it is? Find it.

❧

Do not concern yourself with how long things take. Concern yourself with remaining on the move toward your goal at all times, no matter how slow it might be. As a wonderful Chinese proverb states, "be not afraid of growing slowly, be only afraid of standing still."

❧

Not all days will be productive. It happens! Do not be hard on yourself and take the time to smell the flowers. We all need a break.

❧

Help yourself become someone who is able to help others. Be the hope to others.

There are billions of people on this earth. Become the right woman or the right man, and you will find the right counterpart. Do not sit still. Do not despair. Be positive and active and you will be fine.

❦

You are your own public relations advisor.

❦

Focus more on what you are *doing*, not on what you have not done yet.

❦

At times when you are struggling with something or when you need to accomplish a lot, avoid things that make you sad or depressed.

❦

To get over fear and uncertainty, take it a step at a time. If you don't know where to begin, break the process down into baby steps. Then start moving.

❦

Do not risk everything and do not be selfish. Do not put your family and your savings on the line. Find ways to fulfill your dreams while avoiding hurting others. Do your work legitimately, calmly, actively, and with good intention.

❦

If you want to open up new faculties of your mind, world literature can help.

❦

If you want to improve your creativity and thought process, do free-writing. Sit at a desk with a pen and paper (not a computer) and write on a particular subject for three minutes straight. Do not worry about grammar, spelling or writing perfect sentences. The trick is to **never** take your pen off the page by writing continuously and whatever comes to mind. If you get stuck, write "I don't know what to write." You will see the benefits of this exercise immediately after you are finished.

❀❀

Group activities can help you meet people and develop as a person: salsa and ballroom dancing, martial arts, running clubs, variety clubs, and yoga are great examples. Do not decide you cannot do something before you give yourself the chance to learn.

❀❀

Become a positive force, a legend, in your community. Accept it with Calmness, Intent, Focus, and Humility.

❀❀

Good Luck

❀❀

## YOUR BEGINNING STARTS HERE

❀❀

www.ingramcontent.com/pod-product-compliance
Lightning Source LLC
Chambersburg PA
CBHW020522030426
42337CB00011B/511